BLACK TUESDAY

Prelude to the Great Depression

by Robin S. Doak

BLACK TUESDAY

Prelude to the Great Depression

by Robin S. Doak

Content Adviser: Stephen Asperheim, Ph.D.,
Assistant Professor of History, Savannah State University

Reading Adviser: Alexa L. Sandmann, Ph.D.,
Associate Professor of Literacy, Kent State University

Compass Point Books ✦ Minneapolis, Minnesota

COMPASS POINT BOOKS

3109 West 50th Street, #115
Minneapolis, MN 55410

Visit Compass Point Books on the Internet at
www.compasspointbooks.com
or e-mail your request to
custserv@compasspointbooks.com

For Compass Point Books
Jennifer VanVoorst, Jaime Martens, Lori Bye, XNR Productions, Inc.,
Catherine Neitge, Keith Griffin, and Nick Healy

Produced by White-Thomson Publishing Ltd.

For White-Thomson Publishing
Stephen White-Thomson, Susan Crean, Amy Sparks,
Tinstar Design Ltd., Stephen Asperheim, Peggy Bresnick Kendler,
Barbara Bakowski, and Timothy Griffin

Library of Congress Cataloging-in-Publication Data
Doak, Robin S. (Robin Santos), 1963–
  Black Tuesday : Prelude to the Great Depression / by Robin S. Doak.
    p. cm. — (Snapshots in history)
  ISBN-13: 978-0-7565-3327-4 (library binding)
  ISBN-10: 0-7565-3327-9 (library binding)
1. Stock Market Crash, 1929—Juvenile literature. 2. Depressions—
1929—United States—Juvenile literature. I. Title. II. Series.
  HB37171929 .D63 2008
  330.973'0916—dc22   2007004911

 This book was manufactured with paper containing
at least 10 percent post-consumer waste.

BLACK TUESDAY

CONTENTS

A Black Day

On Tuesday, October 29, 1929, panic erupted in the financial district of New York City. Something had gone very wrong. Stockbrokers were acting strangely. A security guard at the New York Stock Exchange (NYSE) described their behavior that day:

> *They roared like a lot of lions and tigers. They hollered and screamed, they clawed at one another's collars. It was like a bunch of crazy men. Every once in a while, when Radio or Steel or Auburn [stock] would take another tumble, you'd see some poor devil collapse and fall to the floor.*

In the street outside, people crowded in front of the exchange building, pushing and shoving one another to get a closer look at the big building.

Police on horseback kept things under control as thousands of people crowded outside the New York Stock Exchange.

The public viewing gallery inside the exchange had been closed so that visitors would not witness the mayhem taking place there. But as more and more worried investors joined the crowds on Wall Street, the scene outside became nearly as chaotic as the one within. Soon police arrived to make sure that the gathering mob did not get out of hand.

Throughout the 1920s, the NYSE on Wall Street in New York City served as the financial heart of the United States. The exchange floor was where stockbrokers bought and sold shares. It was a symbol of U.S. economic power and wealth. But on Tuesday, October 29, 1929, the U.S. stock market crashed, or collapsed.

Those paying attention saw signs of the coming collapse. On Thursday, October 24, stocks plummeted, but they rebounded the next day. On Tuesday, October 29, thousands of terrified investors were trying to sell their stocks. They wanted to get their money out of the market quickly, before their stocks became worthless. So many orders to sell flooded the stock exchange that stockbrokers couldn't keep up. The ticker tape machines, which were telegraph machines that printed out the latest value of each stock on a piece of paper, were also running behind. This made it nearly impossible for everyone to know just how bad things had become.

Some people had not paid cash for their stocks. They had bought stock with credit, a type of deal

known as margin trading, or buying on margin. These people had expected their stocks to become more valuable. They had planned to pay off their debts to the stockbrokers with the extra money they earned. But now, the value of all of the stocks had dropped, and those in debt were told to pay up. To pay back the loans, some people were forced to wipe out their savings accounts. Others sold china and jewelry to raise the cash to pay their debts. Greek immigrant and South Carolina diner owner George Mehales remembered:

In 1929, traders kept track of stock prices by reading the numbers telegraphed over the ticker tape machine.

11

On that day of October 29, they told me I needed more cash to cover up. I couldn't get it. I was wiped out that day. I guess disappointment comes mighty hard to some people, but that almost killed me. My brother lost in the market like me, and he couldn't help me out. I considered killing myself, 'cause I had nothing left. I found out what a fool I had been. I did manage to pay my debts by selling my cafe at rock-bottom prices. I learned a lesson then. It almost killed me to see my cafe go at such a cheap price.

LIFE IN 1929

Although 1929 would be remembered for October's great stock market crash, many other significant events took place that year.

January 15—Future civil rights activist Martin Luther King Jr. was born in Atlanta.

January 17—The cartoon character Popeye made his debut in the funny pages of newspapers around the nation.

May 16—The first Academy Awards ceremony was held in Hollywood, California. The Best Picture winner was *Wings*, a silent movie about World War I fighter pilots.

June 27—The first demonstration of a color television transmission took place in New York City. Spectators saw a bouquet of roses and an American flag.

September 27—Ernest·Hemingway's classic novel *A Farewell to Arms* was published.

November 29—U.S. explorer Richard Byrd became the first person to fly over the South Pole.

Mehales and thousands of average Americans lost their life savings on that day. Raymond Tarver, a Georgia banker during the crash, said:

> *There were thousands who went down during the panic—lost fortunes, homes, business, and in fact everything. Some have survived, and many never will. A great many were too old to begin building up again.*

Without their savings, some investors chose to end their lives. British politician Winston Churchill was visiting New York during the great crash and was staying with a friend, millionaire Percy Rockefeller. Churchill later recounted a disturbing event that he had witnessed the following day:

> *Under my very window a gentleman cast himself down fifteen storeys [stories] and was dashed to pieces, causing a wild commotion and the arrival of the fire brigade.*

In the coming two years, things would go from bad to worse. Stocks would continue to decrease in value, and by 1932 the United States would be in the grip of the worst economic crisis in its history, the Great Depression. More than a decade of financial hardship was unleashed on the United States with the stock market crash that occurred on October 29, 1929, a day that has come to be known as Black Tuesday.

The Roaring Twenties

Chapter

2

The sudden downturn in the country's financial fortunes that took place in October 1929 marked the end of a turbulent decade. During the 1920s, Americans worked hard to forget the deprivation, death, and destruction that had marked the years during World War I (1914–1918). At the start of the new decade, Republican Senator Warren G. Harding of Ohio won the U.S. presidency by campaigning with the slogan "A Return to Normalcy."

Harding's landslide victory in the 1920 presidential election underscored the appeal of his message. It also highlighted the mood of most Americans at that time. People wanted peace, prosperity, and the return of good times. Author F. Scott Fitzgerald wrote:

Warren G. Harding, elected by a landslide, accomplished little as president and chose several corrupt men to advise him. After his death, a number of scandals that took place during his presidency came to light.

> *The uncertainties of 1919 were over—there seemed little doubt about what was going to happen—America was going on the greatest, gaudiest [flashiest] spree in history.*

Before long, this new decade—filled with change, excitement, and general prosperity—was known as the Roaring Twenties.

Although Americans were ready for a party at the start of the 1920s, people in favor of the 18th Amendment to the U.S. Constitution tried to make sure that the party was alcohol-free. Passed in 1920, the 18th Amendment made Prohibition the law of the land. Many Americans initially supported the ban on the manufacture and sale of alcoholic beverages. They believed that alcohol use—especially by recent immigrants—led to poverty, sickness, and a loosening of morals and behavior.

F. SCOTT FITZGERALD

Novelist F. Scott Fitzgerald and his wife, Zelda, came to symbolize both the brilliance and the excess of the Roaring Twenties. Fitzgerald was the acclaimed author of *This Side of Paradise* and *The Great Gatsby*. In his work, Fitzgerald chronicled the glittering yet empty lives of the rich. His writing created a snapshot of the 1920s, highlighting the decade's optimism as well as its underlying despair. Fitzgerald became known as the voice of the "Lost Generation," the generation of young people living in America after World War I and before the Great Depression.

The law was well intentioned, but it ultimately caused more harm than good. Americans who wanted to drink alcohol found ways to do so, even if it meant breaking the law. Some made their own liquor. Others patronized speakeasies and "blind pigs," illegal bars where they could enjoy a drink while listening to the latest musical craze, jazz.

Federal, state, and local officials, such as New York Deputy Police Commissioner John A. Leach (right), enforced Prohibition by seizing and destroying illegal alcohol.

17

The Prohibition era also saw the rise of bootleggers, criminals who made, transported, and sold liquor. Gangs sprang up in cities such as Chicago and New York, with members battling one another for the privilege of being the only alcohol supplier on their turf.

No single group experienced greater change during the 1920s than women. In 1920, the 19th Amendment to the U.S. Constitution also went into effect. This amendment gave women across the nation the right to vote. Women had finally won the right to fully participate in politics and the democratic process.

After earning equal rights in the voting booth, American women now began to demand equality in other areas. Women carved out a bold new role for themselves in the society of the 1920s. Young women began cutting their hair, shortening their skirts, and wearing makeup. They also visited speakeasies, danced to jazz music, and smoked cigarettes.

THE KING OF THE BOOTLEGGERS

One of the most infamous bootleggers of the 1920s was Al Capone. He was born to Italian immigrants in Brooklyn, New York, in 1899. Capone began his criminal career after he dropped out of school in sixth grade to join a boys' gang. In 1920, at the age of 21, he relocated to Chicago. In just five years, he took control of the city's illegal alcohol, gambling, and prostitution businesses. Capone was willing to do whatever it took to keep control of his multimillion-dollar empire, including bribing politicians, putting policemen on his payroll, and killing rivals.

This new style of woman became known as the flapper. Flappers demanded equality at home,

in the workplace, and in every other area of U.S. society.

As the hemlines of skirts and dresses climbed ever higher, so did the tempers of parents and those who wanted to preserve the good old days of

During a parade in New York City in 1915, thousands of women called for the right to vote.

19

corsets and long dresses. Some Americans felt that the "new woman" of the 1920s heralded a decline in the entire moral fabric of the United States. The Women's Christian Temperance Union issued this

Flapper fashions showcased higher hemlines and lower necklines.

statement: "No nation can maintain the vigor which has been characteristic of the American people after its women begin the use of cigarettes."

But not all Americans condemned the flappers as the end of American civilization. In 1924, Chicago's public health commissioner penned these words about the "new woman":

> *Then came a few bolder spirits who decided that a head of unwashed hair, difficult to manage, was not necessarily a 'crowning glory' and so they began bobbing it. Some girls dared to don knickers, put on stout shoes, and take long hikes.*

> *Did these acts make them less womanly? Does bobbed hair make a woman a worse housewife or prospective mother? We do not think so. …*

> *All of these innovations simply mean the emancipation of girlhood and womanhood from the old idea that women must be one thing and men another. It simply means that woman is advancing to the place in which she rightly belongs; that she is capable of performing not only her own work, but can compete with her brother in the ordinary routine of life.*

The social revolution of the 1920s also led to a backlash of racism and anti-immigrant sentiment. Some people blamed the changes in society on the increasing presence of minority and immigrant

During the 1920s, the number of people allowed to immigrate to the United States from Japan and other parts of Asia was drastically cut.

groups in the United States. And some people were willing to speak and act out against those they considered "un-American." In the early 1920s, for example, the hate group known as the Ku Klux Klan (KKK) grew stronger. KKK members targeted African-Americans, Jews, immigrants, and Catholics with their hate.

In keeping with the anti-immigration sentiment felt by many Americans, the U.S. Congress passed strict immigration laws in 1924. The laws cut the number of people allowed to immigrate to the United States from certain regions, especially Asia and Eastern Europe.

For conservative Americans, a return to normalcy meant holding tight to the customs and values of past generations, including religion. In 1925, religion was at the center of the Scopes trial, popularly known as the "Monkey Trial." High school teacher John Scopes was put on trial in Tennessee for teaching the theory of evolution, a scientific concept that differed from the teachings of the Bible. Scopes was found guilty and fined but was later acquitted. ◣

The Business of America

Within a few years of President Harding's promise for a return to normalcy, the country began to bounce back from the effects of World War I. However, Harding himself had little to do with the economic recovery of the United States. The president told close friends that he was unqualified to run the nation, and he was right. Advisers and government officials took advantage of the chief executive, and his term in office would eventually produce little but scandals.

On August 2, 1923, an ailing President Harding died unexpectedly in San Francisco. He was 58 years old. Harding's vice president, Calvin Coolidge, was quickly sworn in as the nation's 30th president.

Calvin Coolidge was sworn in to office by his father, a justice of the peace, at the general store in Plymouth Notch, New Hampshire. Coolidge and his family were vacationing there when President Harding died.

As president, Coolidge's top priority was to continue the recovery that the U.S. economy had begun under Harding. As a Republican, the new president believed that the best way to help the economy flourish was to leave it alone. This philosophy is known as laissez-faire economics. He believed that the government should not place too many restrictions on private businesses. Government regulatory agencies, Coolidge believed, should aid businesses, not police them. Near the end of his time in office, Coolidge told reporters, "Perhaps one of the most important accomplishments of my administration has been minding my own business." During his presidency, the U.S. economy thrived as never before.

When Coolidge ran for a full term as president in 1924, he campaigned under the slogans "Coolidge

LAISSEZ-FAIRE ECONOMICS

Laissez-faire economics is the principle of keeping government out of business and industry as much as possible. *Laissez-faire*, from the French phrase for "let it be," was the perfect way to describe President Coolidge's view on most issues throughout his presidency. Coolidge imposed few regulations on big industries in the United States. He also vetoed bills passed by Congress that would have aided veterans and farmers. And when it came to foreign policy, Coolidge preferred to not get involved in the affairs of other nations. After the Great Crash, editors at *Business Week* would mock Coolidge's laissez-faire policies. In June 1931, the magazine ran a story with the title "Do You Still Believe in Lazy-Fairies?"

Prosperity" and "Keep Cool with Coolidge." Like Harding, Coolidge beat his opponents in a landslide. In his inauguration speech, Coolidge had a positive message for Americans. He said, "Business has revived, and we appear to be entering into an era of prosperity which is gradually reaching into every part of the nation."

Most Americans agreed with the president. When Coolidge took office, the U.S. economy was booming, and Americans felt richer than ever before. For the next four years, mass-produced goods and consumer spending on a huge scale powered the economy. Coolidge summed it up in a 1925 speech: "The chief business of the American people is business. They are profoundly concerned with producing, buying, selling, investing, and prospering in the world."

The booming U.S. economy was made possible by two important advancements: the spread of electricity and mass production. During the 1920s, electricity powered more and more of the nation's factories, increasing productivity. Electricity also affected the average American: In 1912, only 16 percent of U.S. homes were wired for electricity, but by 1927 that number had risen to 63 percent. People with electricity at home could now buy the latest in modern household appliances, including radios, washing machines, refrigerators, toasters, vacuum cleaners, and telephones. Mass production provided the goods that the middle-class American consumer purchased in large quantities. U.S. industries were now more productive than ever before.

To make sure that Americans purchased the mass-produced goods, two new industries arose as well: advertising and sales. Copywriters and artists created images of the ideal American— one with perfect skin and hair, fresh breath, and no body odor. This image, they promised, could be a reality if Americans bought the right products.

Chain stores and department stores took over from neighborhood shops as the places to purchase the latest fads and newest necessities. Owners of small shops were unable to compete with larger stores that sold a wide variety of goods at lower prices. Shopkeepers quickly learned that the new, mobile American was willing to drive a few miles to browse the big stores' aisles.

THE BIRTH OF MASS PRODUCTION

In 1905, Henry Ford made mass production a reality when he perfected the assembly line in his automobile factory. On Ford's assembly line, each worker was given one specific task to perform. After the first worker finished his task, the next worker did his part, and so on until the automobile was finished. The assembly line reduced the need for skilled workers and sped up the process of making one car. The assembly line allowed automobiles to be produced far more cheaply and quickly than ever before. By the 1920s, many other industries had copied Ford's successful assembly line technique, and large supplies of products were soon being shipped out of factories to consumers across the United States.

If a person did not have the ready cash necessary to buy a brand-new radio, refrigerator, or automobile, that was no problem. The 1920s also marked the beginning of the practice of buying on credit. Each week or month, the purchaser paid the seller part of the total owed—plus a little extra. The extra was to pay off the interest, or fee, charged by the seller for the loan.

In 1926, the National Association of Credit Men pointed out the dangers of buying on credit:

Making it easy for people to buy beyond their needs or to buy before they have saved enough to gratify their wishes tends to encourage a condition that hurts the human morale.

The advertising industry boomed during the 1920s as companies competed for consumer dollars.

Of all the goods purchased by people during the decade, the automobile was the most influential and the most important. Ford, Oldsmobile, General Motors, Cadillac, Chevrolet, and many other manufacturers made cars. Between 1919 and 1929, the number of automobiles on the road more than tripled, rising to more than 26 million.

The popularity of the motorcar boosted various secondary industries, such as gas, rubber, and steel. Food stands, camping sites, and gas stations sprang up along new, freshly paved roads and highways to serve travelers. One historian later estimated that nearly 4 million Americans were employed in automobile or automobile-related work.

Henry Ford's inexpensive Model T was the most popular car in the United States. By 1927, Ford had manufactured 15 million cars. For many years, the Model T was produced only in black to speed up assembly time.

A New Status Symbol

During the 1920s, the automobile became a status symbol—an item that everyone who was anyone had to have. In 1925, William Ashdown wrote in "Confessions of an Automobilist" in *Atlantic Monthly* magazine: "Dangerous rivalries among friends and in families are created by the motor. If one member of a family makes a bit of money he must advertise it to the rest of the family and to the world by the purchase of a car. Or, if his social scale seems a bit below that of the rest of the family, he seeks to lift himself higher through the medium of a car. The result is a costly rivalry that brings the whole group into debt."

The automobile also changed U.S. settlement patterns. As Americans became more mobile, they began moving out of the cities and into suburbs. The era of commuting to work had begun.

With increased productivity, business owners were willing to give workers a shorter workweek. By the end of the 1920s, the average number of hours worked weekly in U.S. factories had decreased from 60 to 48. The average earnings of an American worker had increased by 22 percent. Americans now had leisure time—and money—to spare. And they quickly found ways to fill their idle hours. One journalist, Robert L. Duffus, dubbed the 1920s the Age of Play.

Not all Americans were able to enjoy the Age of Play, however. Cracks were beginning to appear in the U.S. economy, and the gap between rich and

poor people was widening. Unemployment was
creeping upward, and for those without jobs, life
was not so much fun.

Even so, many Americans had a good deal of
disposable income, which they happily spent

*Men and women
took advantage
of more leisure
time and spending
money to socialize
and have fun.*

on luxuries like entertainment. The latest forms of entertainment—radio and motion pictures—opened up new worlds for people across the nation. In the past, only the wealthy were able to attend plays, operas, and balls. Now all Americans could hear and see what they had been missing.

Silent movie comedian Charlie Chaplin was one of the most popular actors in Hollywood. His 1925 movie The Gold Rush *is considered a cinema classic.*

By the mid-1920s, most homes in the United States had a radio. Radio stations such as the National Broadcasting Company and the Columbia Broadcasting System aired news, music, and comedy shows. And throughout most of the 1920s, silent movies attracted people of all social classes

THE LONE EAGLE

During the 1920s, Americans yearned for adventure and excitement, and their heroes were often men and women who performed feats of bravery and daring. One of the most famous people of the era was Charles Lindbergh, a handsome and daring young aviator. In 1927, Lindbergh became the first person to cross the Atlantic solo by plane. On May 20 of that year, the 25-year-old Minnesota native left New York in the *Spirit of St. Louis*, a small monoplane that he had helped design. When he arrived in Paris 33½ hours later, he was greeted by thousands of cheering admirers.

to movie theaters. Men, women, and children could relax and enjoy westerns, dramas, and comedies featuring movie stars such as Tom Mix, Mary Pickford, and Charlie Chaplin.

In 1929, the addition of sound to the movies would make cinemas even more popular with Americans. In the coming years, the Hollywood movie industry would become a major moneymaker as more and more Americans paid to see the latest films featuring their favorite stars. ◣

Gambling on the Stock Market

The 1920s was a decade of unparalleled economic growth. Many Americans had more time and money than ever before. They also had a strong belief that the U.S. economy would continue to boom. Many Americans gambled on the continued strength of the economy by investing in the stock market.

After World War I, the acknowledged financial center of the United States—and the world—was New York City. Lower Manhattan was home to more than 90 banks, as well as many insurance companies, corporate headquarters, and financial firms. But the most important spot in the city was undoubtedly the New York Stock Exchange, located at Broad and Wall streets. The prosperity and strength of the U.S. economy was mirrored in the success of the NYSE.

The New York Stock Exchange building opened in 1903. Today the building at 18 Broad St. is on the National Register of Historic Places.

37

Although there were other stock exchanges in New York, around the nation, and throughout the world, none had the prestige of the NYSE. Monday through Friday, hundreds of stockbrokers crowded onto the trading floor, waiting for the big brass bell to signal the beginning of trading at 10 A.M. During the mid-1920s, about 4 million shares of stock were traded each day before the closing bell at 3 P.M. On Saturday, brokers worked a shortened day, from 10 A.M. until noon.

In order to trade on the NYSE floor, a broker had to purchase one of 1,100 seats on the exchange. (The number of seats was increased to 1,375 in February 1929.) Most of the seats were owned by brokerage firms, but others were owned by individuals. In November 1928, the price of each seat was $580,000, a small fortune at the time. Each stockbroker then bought or sold stock, as directed by his clients. There were no women stockbrokers in the NYSE until decades later.

THE BIRTH OF THE NEW YORK STOCK EXCHANGE

In 1792, a group of 24 brokers and merchants met beneath a buttonwood tree on Wall Street in New York City. There the men signed the Buttonwood Agreement, committing to trade securities with one another. The same year, the Bank of New York became the first stock listed under the Buttonwood Agreement. In March 1817, the trading group was formally named the New York Stock and Exchange Board, which became the New York Stock Exchange (NYSE) 46 years later. Although the NYSE quickly became the most important stock market in the nation, it wasn't the first. Philadelphia's stock exchange was founded in 1790, two years before the birth of the NYSE.

On any given day, the NYSE was bustling with activity. Brokers bought and sold while board boys, also known as chalkies, hustled back and forth, reading the ever-running ticker tape and chalking the numbers onto large boards. Pages, clerks, and telephone operators were also part of the day-to-day bustle. Even tourists stopped by, watching from the viewing section to witness firsthand the business of making money.

The value of each company's stock was based on whatever price buyers were willing to pay for

After the opening bell chimed, the trading floor on the New York Stock Exchange was a busy place.

39

it in the open market. If investors believed that a company was growing larger and stronger, the company's stock probably rose. The stock price of a poorly managed company that was having financial woes, however, usually dropped. Most investors tried to follow the old financial maxim "Buy Low, Sell High," in order to make the greatest profits.

As the stock market got stronger, average Americans thought they saw a way to get rich quickly. By the late 1920s, almost everyone seemed to know of someone who had made a fortune by gambling on the rise and fall of stocks. Men and women from all walks of life began using their extra money to gamble on the stock market. Most had faith that the U.S. economy was only going to get stronger. And they were willing to place their hard-earned money on this faith.

In 1928, writer Robert Ryan described the average small-time investor:

THE TICKER TAPE PARADE

Since the late 1800s, New Yorkers have been celebrating important events by throwing pieces of cut-up paper from ticker tape machines. The first ticker tape parade was held on October 29, 1886, after the dedication of the Statue of Liberty in New York Harbor. The event started off as an ordinary parade, but excited office workers leaned out of windows and threw the paper like confetti. In June 1927, pilot Charles Lindbergh was honored with a parade after he returned from making his famous solo flight to Paris. About 750,000 pounds (337,500 kilograms) of ticker tape filled the air. Today ticker tape has been replaced by shredded white paper.

The ranks of the inexperienced—the 'suckers'—were swelled by numbers of men who had been attracted by newspaper stories of the big easy profits to be made, ... of millions captured overnight. ... At first these newcomers risked a few hundred dollars with some broker they knew, discovered that it was easy to make money this way, and finally made their headquarters in the broker's large customer's room, bringing with them their entire checking and savings accounts.

At first, most people seemed to be rewarded by their faith in the stock market. After a slow start in 1928, stock values quickly rebounded. In early March, the market entered its most profitable period ever. Values of individual stocks skyrocketed, and the volume of stocks traded each day increased rapidly, climbing to more than 5 million. Although many experts were astounded at—and concerned about—the new levels, many Americans felt that things would continue to boom. Financial experts fueled that opinion, believing that new technology stocks like radio would keep the market afloat.

THE ERA OF THE SKYSCRAPER

One sign of New York's importance as a financial center was the height of its skyscrapers. The building boom started in the early 1900s, when available space in the city's business districts started to become scarce. To remedy the problem, builders began building upward, and as the years passed, the offices, stores, and hotels of New York became taller and taller. In the early 1920s, construction boomed, and 20-story buildings became common. By the end of the decade, 19 buildings with 40 or more stories had drastically altered the city's skyline.

41

Americans were encouraged to invest their money in stocks by some of the nation's top financiers. John J. Raskob, vice president of General Motors, wrote an article for *Ladies' Home Journal* in August 1929. In the article, titled "Everybody Ought to Be Rich," he encouraged Americans to save $15 a month to invest in stocks. This was not an easy task: Most Americans earned just $100 a month. He told readers that speculators who let their money add up would eventually be wealthy:

> *Anyone who firmly believes that the opportunities are all closed and that from now on the country will get worse instead of better*

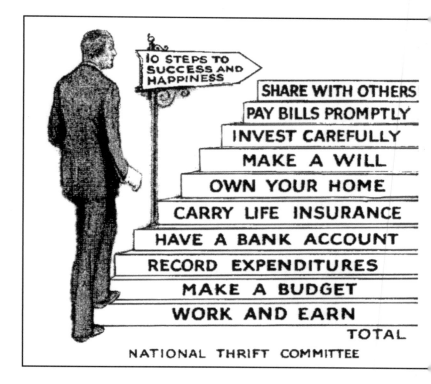

is welcome to the opinion. ... I think that we have scarcely started, and I have thought so for many years. ... If he [an average 23-year-old man] invests in good common stocks and allows the dividends and rights to accumulate, he will at the end of twenty years have at least eighty thousand dollars and an income from investments of around four hundred dollars a month. He will be rich. And because anyone can do that I am firm in my belief that anyone not only can be rich but ought to be rich.

No one knows exactly how many small investors throughout the United States invested in stocks in the mid- and late 1920s. But even those who did not

PERFECT SCORE	MY SCORE
10%	
10%	
10%	
10%	
10%	
10%	
10%	
10%	
10%	
10%	
100%	

Will your present money methods take you to Success and Happiness? If you follow the ten rules both will be yours. Measure Yourself. If you score 100% you are safe. Just 10 Steps.
BEGIN NOW

347 MADISON AVE., NEW YORK, N.Y.

Although many Americans were spending money as never before, organizations such as the National Thrift Committee warned people to be cautious.

43

invest became obsessed with watching the dramatic rise of U.S. stocks. People bought the afternoon newspapers just to read the financial pages. Others dropped by their local broker's office to watch the latest prices roll out of the ticker tape machine.

During the 1920s, the public enjoyed tracking stock prices from day to day in The New York Times *and other newspapers.*

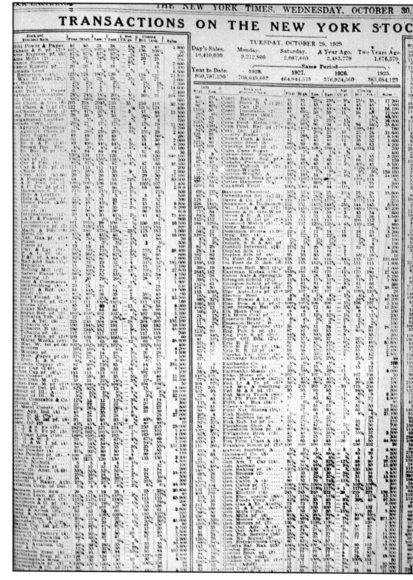

The stock market might have seemed like an easy way to get rich quickly, but it was not. Alex Samuels, a college professor who made some money trading in stocks, said:

> *Trading stocks is not a job that is suitable to many. It requires very careful study. A person attempting to trade on a little newspaper opinion and so-called expert advice is almost certain to have serious losses. The reason is not hard to see. ... The only people I have ever known who made money consistently were those who formed their own opinions and made a business of their trading. A great many people who would not think of playing against professionals for money in a card game will attempt to speculate. They are playing a far more complicated game in competition with very shrewd opponents.*

From Prosperity to Peril

In the late 1920s, business was strong, the stock market was booming, and Americans were, on the whole, better off than they had been shortly after the war. Most people would have agreed that President Coolidge's laissez-faire policies had served the nation well. Americans expected that Coolidge would run for a second full term and that the economy would continue to thrive. So when the president announced in August 1927 that he would not seek re-election, people across the country were shocked.

When Coolidge's secretary of commerce, Herbert Hoover, was chosen by Republicans to run for the presidency, he expected to win. As he campaigned throughout the United States in 1928, he referred to the prosperity people enjoyed under Coolidge and forecast a rosy future:

Herbert Hoover was highly qualified to become president of the United States. He had served as secretary of commerce under two presidents.

We in America today are nearer to the final triumph over poverty than ever before in the history of any land. The poorhouse is vanishing from among us. ...We shall soon, with the help of God, be in sight of the day when poverty will be banished from this nation.

With Republicans promising a chicken in every pot and a car in every garage, Hoover—as predicted—easily won the election.

As Hoover prepared to take over the presidency, however, signs of trouble were evident. Calvin Coolidge's laissez-faire policy had done serious damage to the U.S. economy. Unemployment was high, and the gap between rich and poor people grew wider every year.

Some groups of workers had not prospered at all in the 1920s. Wheat, corn, and cotton farmers, for example, had continued to suffer since the end of the war. They asked for help from the government, and in 1927 the Farm Relief Bill was passed by Congress. However, Coolidge vetoed the bill, in keeping with his belief that government should not interfere with private businesses. As a result, hundreds of thousands of people gave up farming and moved to the cities to find work.

Without any real government regulation, the NYSE had serious problems of its own. In the late 1920s, more Americans than ever before were purchasing stocks on credit. By 1927, banks had loaned stockbrokers more than $3.5 billion, which

they in turn used to cover the costs of heavy margin trading. The brokers liked buying stocks on margin for their small clients. They could charge a substantial fee for these loans. Such loans were known as call loans because they could be called in, or collected, at any time.

American farmers were suffering in the mid-1920s.

49

To people who believed that the market would continue to skyrocket, there seemed to be little risk involved. Every time the market had plummeted, it had come back stronger than ever before. In an interview with writer Studs Terkel, advertising agent Arthur A. Robertson remembered, "I saw shoeshine boys buying $50,000 worth of stock with $500 down. Everything was bought on hope."

Telephone operators on the exchange floor called clients with the latest stock prices.

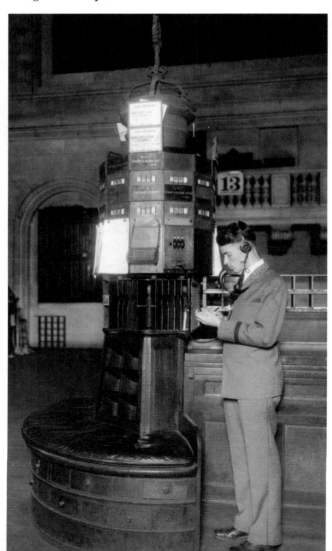

Another problem with the stock exchange was the increase in the number of investment trusts. They catered to Americans who were not confident in choosing which stocks to buy. Instead, these amateur traders could buy stock in a company whose sole purpose was investing money in other companies. The company did not have to tell customers what stocks they were buying or how their money had been invested. Although most of the earliest investment trusts were reputable, this changed over time. Corrupt financiers saw an opportunity to make money by taking advantage of new investors.

Some experts believed that the values of many stocks were grossly inflated. However, sometimes the price a stock traded for had little connection to the company's actual worth. (A stock's real value is based on the value of a company and its expected future earnings.) For example, Commonwealth Edison traded for $35 at its highest point in 1929. It was actually worth only $3.31. Because of the lack of government controls, companies could print out as many stock certificates as they wanted. Although these experts often warned investors to use caution when buying stock, few people listened.

The stock market continued to break records. In late 1928 and early 1929, the Federal Reserve Board stepped in, hoping to cool the market down. The agency raised interest rates, the fees charged to borrow money, hoping to discourage people from borrowing money and speculating on stocks.

The Federal Reserve

In 1913, President Woodrow Wilson created the Federal Reserve Board to regulate the banking industry. The Reserve's goal was to create a stable financial and monetary system in the nation. All U.S. banks were required to join the agency and to invest 3 percent of their money in one of the 12 regional Reserve banks. During the presidency of Calvin Coolidge, Reserve officials were encouraged to aid, not oversee, banking. Many historians believe that Reserve policies helped briefly depress the economy after World War I and contributed to the Great Depression that began after the 1929 stock market crash. Over the years, the agency's practices have been fine-tuned. Today the Federal Reserve is still the chief regulatory agency of the U.S. banking industry.

The rate increase did not have the intended effect. Worried about a weakening economy, individuals and companies stopped buying certain items. As a result, industries slowed production of materials and goods, and the United States entered a mild recession, a temporary slowing of business activity.

However, Americans continued to invest in the stock market, even as stock values climbed to record highs. As long as investors believed the U.S. economy would stay strong, they kept putting money into the stock market. They believed that the price of stocks—even those that were already high—would continue to rise.

After Hoover's inauguration on March 4, 1929, the stock market began a wild roller-coaster ride. That month, stock values dropped, and more than

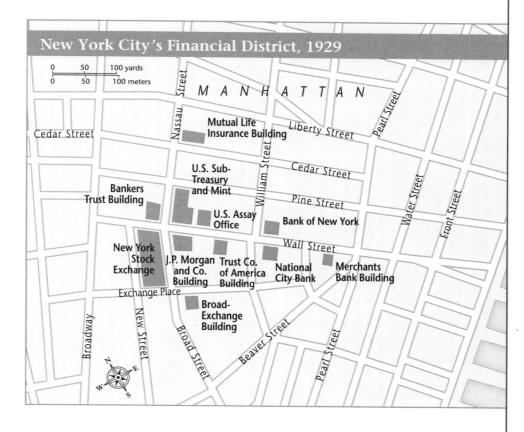

New York City's Financial District, 1929

8 million shares changed hands on just one day. Soon values climbed again as people continued to pour money into the market. In May, stocks fell again, but they recovered by June.

By 1929, Wall Street in New York City had long been the center of the U.S. finance industry.

By the summer of 1929, the stock market seemed stronger and healthier than ever before. An estimated 1 million Americans had bought stock on margin. An even larger number owned stock that they had purchased with their own money. In October, many of these investors would lose everything. ◣

The Panic Begins

As the summer of 1929 drew to a close, the stock market became more unstable than ever. On September 3, the average value of certain select stocks, known as the Dow Jones average, reached an all-time high. Within a year and a half, many large stocks had more than doubled in value. One of the biggest gainers, Radio Corporation of America, had seen its stock price rise by 500 percent since March 3, 1928. Most Americans believed that stock values would rise even higher. Astrologer Evangeline Adams, fortuneteller to the stars, prophesied that the stock market could "climb to heaven."

Then, on September 5, stock values plummeted. Some people traced the decline to a speech by Roger Babson at the National Business College. He was one of few experts to speak negatively

People anxiously scanned newspapers for word of what was happening with the value of their stocks.

about the stock market, and he may have scared investors with his frank words:

Fair weather cannot always continue. ... More people are borrowing and speculating today than ever in our history. Some day the time is coming when the market will begin to slide off, sellers will exceed buyers, and paper profits will begin to disappear. Then there will be an immediate stampede to save what paper profits then exist.

The September 5 drop—the first serious drop in the stock market—became known as the "Babson Break."

Instead of taking their money out of the stock market at the first sign of trouble, many Americans saw the drop as a chance to buy stock at bargain prices. After all, stocks had dipped before, but they had always recovered and climbed to new highs. By mid-September 1929, it seemed that the speculators were right. Stocks again climbed to record highs. Few people

STOCKS AHOY!

Stockbroker Michael Meehan had purchased a seat on the New York Stock Exchange in 1920. By 1929, Meehan's firm, M.J. Meehan & Company, owned eight seats, more than any other financial house. In August 1929, Meehan opened up the first brokerage onboard a ship. That month, floating branches of M.J. Meehan & Company were set up on the promenade deck of the *Berengaria* and in the tearoom of the *Leviathan*. The branch on the *Leviathan* included a board with room for 20 stocks and lounge chairs for potential investors. Stock quotes were transmitted from Meehan's office by radio.

realized, however, that the stocks had reached their limit. The stock market would not reach such levels again until the 1950s.

By the beginning of October, stocks had again begun to decline. Yet the amount of money loaned by banks to brokers for margin purchases soared, reaching a record of $6.8 billion. It seemed that nothing would deter Americans from investing in the stock market. Financial experts assured them that their money was safe.

On October 16, just days before the events occurred that would send the United States—and the rest of the world—into a financial panic, the *Boston News Bureau* reported, "Business is too big and diversified, and the country too rich, to be influenced by the stock-market fluctuations." The following day, as stocks rose again, professor Irving Fisher of Yale University stated: "Stocks have reached what looks like a permanently high plateau."

Then, just days before the panic, stocks dipped to their lowest levels yet. R.W. McNeel, the director of McNeel's Financial Service, said to the *Boston News Bureau:*

> *Some pretty intelligent people are now buying stocks. ... Unless we are to have a panic— which no one seriously believes—stocks have hit bottom.*

But some experts warned American investors that the outlook was not good. In early October, the Standard Trade and Securities Service told clients, "We remain of the opinion that, over the next few months, the trend of common-stock prices will be toward lower levels." However, the positive predictions far outweighed the warnings to prepare for worse to come.

On Wednesday, October 23, 1929, Americans finally seemed to realize that the market would not recover from its most recent dip. That day thousands of investors began selling off their stocks, hoping to save some of their investments. Throughout the day, more than 6 million shares were traded, and the ticker tape ran an hour and a half behind.

KNOWING WHEN TO SELL

Some investors saved their family fortunes by quietly selling off their stocks before the autumn of 1929. One such person was Joseph P. Kennedy, the father of future U.S. President John F. Kennedy. The elder Kennedy began worrying about his investments in July 1929, when stocks were still at record highs. Although financial experts counseled him to keep his money in the market, the wealthy Boston native decided otherwise. He sold off his stocks and avoided ruin in October. Another well-known person who sold his stocks before the panic was Will Rogers, a famous entertainer. Although Rogers wanted to buy stocks, his financier friend Bernard Baruch counseled against it: "You're sitting on a volcano. That's all right for professional volcano sitters like myself, but an amateur like you ought to ... get as far away as possible."

As the values of stocks plummeted, stockbrokers called their clients who had bought stocks on margin with some bad news: Their stocks were no longer worth the money they had borrowed and paid for them. To cover their loans, clients had to come up with even more money to cover

As stock prices dropped, traders rushed to the phones to ask investors for cash to cover margin loans.

59

the loss in value. If the client couldn't come up with the cash, the broker could sell the stocks without permission.

October 24, known as Black Thursday, was even worse than the day before. On that day, 12,894,650 shares changed hands. At first most of the stocks

were dumped by stockbrokers who had held them for margin clients who could no longer pay for them. Later, as word spread of the massive sell-off, more investors became frightened and sold their stocks as well.

The scene on the stock exchange floor was one of panic, especially as the day wore on and the market continued to drop. Telephone lines were jammed as orders to sell and requests for information flooded stockbrokers on the floor. But the brokers had few answers. Again, the ticker tape had fallen far behind the most recent selling information.

Frightened investors streamed into their brokers' customer offices, clamoring for information about their investments. As brokers rushed frantically around the stock exchange floor, shouting and sweating, huge crowds gathered outside on Wall Street. Police officers moved in to maintain order, while news reporters and photographers recorded the scene. Rumors spread through the crowd that 11 investors, having lost their savings after spending the money on stocks, had committed suicide.

Shortly before noon, a group of the most important men on Wall Street met to determine what might be done to stop the avalanche of stock prices. In an effort to stem the panic, these bankers and financiers pledged $40 million to help keep the stock market from totally collapsing. The money would be used to purchase stocks in the hopes of instilling some confidence in investors. After the meeting, Thomas Lamont, of J.P. Morgan & Company, told reporters:

> *There has been a little distress on the stock market. … We have found that there are no houses in difficulty, and reports from brokers indicate that margins are being maintained satisfactorily.*

The infusion of cash helped. Prices evened out, and people began phoning in orders to buy. Even with the brief recovery, however, the day's damage had already been done. The market had dropped 21 percent from its high in early September, and a record 12.9 million shares of stock had been traded.

The panic on Black Thursday was front-page news—but worse was yet to come.

World

FINAL NEWS EDITION

Market in Panic as Stocks Are Dumped in 12,894,600 Share Day; Bankers Halt It

Board Meets.
Mellon Sitting
Announces No Ac-
Rumors of Rate Cut

HOWEVER, FINDS
CONDITIONS SOUND

New Cries in Chorus
Investigation

Outside J. P. Morgan & Co.

Halts Decline in
Day's Disorder
on Stock Exchange

EXPERTS TERM COLLAPSE
SPECULATIVE PHENOMENON

Effect Is Felt in the Curb and
Throughout Nations—Finan-

The ticker tape machine did not stop working until after 7 P.M. that evening.

After Black Thursday, government officials and financial experts spoke out, hoping to calm Americans and play down the serious nature of the day's panic. On Friday, President Hoover said that U.S. business was in good shape:

> *The fundamental business of the country, that is, production and distribution of commodities, is on a sound and prosperous basis.*

In the days following Black Thursday, financial experts stepped forward with comments tailored to boost the confidence of American investors. Arthur W. Loasby, president of the Equitable Trust Company, chimed in:

> *There will be no repetition of the break of yesterday. The market fell of its own weight, without regard to fundamental business conditions, which are sound. I have no fear of another comparable decline.*

And J.L. Julian, a partner in the Fenner and Beane financial firm, said:

> *The worst is over. The selling yesterday was panicky brought on by hysteria. General conditions are good. Our inquiries assure us that throughout the country business is sound.*

On October 26, *The New York Times* reported reassuring words from Wall Street heavyweights, saying, "The spasm of fear which accompanied Thursday's unsettlement … was overcome more speedily than it developed."

Following Black Thursday, worried investors flooded Wall Street.

On the same day, the Harvard Economic Society issued a statement:

> *Despite its severity, we believe that the slump in stock prices will prove an intermediate movement and not the precursor of a business depression.*

At first, all the talk seemed to pay off, and the market held steady on Friday. During the short trading session on Saturday, the stock market continued to look stable. Some of the people who had panicked on Thursday had even begun buying again. Most Americans felt that the market could not go any lower—that the bottom had dropped out. But the worst day of all was still to come. ◣

A Bleak Week

The market's stability on the Friday and Saturday following Black Thursday was deceptive. On Monday, October 28, investors once again started selling off large amounts of stock. That day, 9.2 million shares were traded. One-third of the stocks were traded in the last hour of business, a sign of things to come the following day.

Almost as soon as the opening bell sounded on Tuesday, the avalanche of selling started up again as brokerage firms, banks, and companies dumped huge blocks of stock onto the market. Once again, telephone and telegraph lines were flooded with calls from panicked investors, ordering their brokers to sell at any price. In the first half hour, 3 million shares were traded.

Crowds gathered around the New York Stock Exchange building following the stock market crash on Black Tuesday.

Again, panic ruled the stock market. But this time, the panic was worse than in the days before. All over the country, people—even those who had already lost their fortunes—crowded into brokers' offices. Everyone wanted to see firsthand the unbelievable events taking place on Wall Street.

So many people gathered outside the stock exchange during the crash that police were called in to control the crowd.

In Lower Manhattan, people jostled to be near the exchange building as the market crashed. Police were called to make sure that the gathering crowds didn't get out of hand. Around the nation, people waited anxiously for news of what was going on.

Was the market recovering, as it had in the past? Or should they dump their stocks, as everyone else seemed to be doing?

The front page of *The New York Times* reported, "Wall Street was a street of vanished hopes, of curiously silent apprehension and a sort of paralyzed hypnosis yesterday." Inside, the *Times* further described the scene:

> *The crowds about the ticker tapes, like friends about the bedside of a stricken friend, reflected in their faces the story the tape was telling. There were no smiles. There were no tears either. ... Everybody wanted to tell his neighbor how much he had lost. Nobody wanted to listen. It was too repetitious a tale.*

SEXISM IN 1929

After Black Tuesday, *The New York Times* featured an article about the reaction of women to the stock market crash. The story highlighted the attitude that many men still had toward women in 1929. It included descriptions of some of the "irritable and nervous" women traders the reporter saw during the course of the day: "Stock brokers have said that the women speculators are the worst losers. ... They pushed their way into the crowded rooms, asked for the latest quotations and then blamed the brokers for the condition of things." The men in the story received better treatment. The reporter wrote, "The men in the uptown offices gathered around the tickers, sat quietly in their chairs or stood along the walls of the room. They made calculations, they appeared worried, but they said very little."

Fearing that closing the stock exchange would cause even greater panic in the days to come, the NYSE's Governing Committee left the market open. The bankers who had helped stem the panic the previous Thursday by buying $40 million worth of stocks met and concluded that they could do nothing to stop the day's market collapse. The Federal Reserve also met and decided to let the panic run its course.

The United States had never before witnessed such a massive sell-off of stocks. Never before had investors panicked on such a large scale. By the end of the day known as Black Tuesday, 16.4 million shares had changed hands—a record for the number of shares traded in a single day. The entire week, beginning on October 23, was disastrous. During the eight days that the stock market was open between October 23 and October 31, 70.8 million shares changed hands. The NYSE wasn't the only exchange affected. Around the United States and the world, stock markets took heavy losses. Markets in Philadelphia, Boston, Chicago, Montreal, London, and other cities all suffered.

STOCKS IN THE GARBAGE

After the closing bell put an end to Black Tuesday, one Wall Street broker realized that he had a trash can stuffed with unfulfilled orders to buy and sell. During the day's most chaotic moments, the man had stuffed the orders into the wastebasket, hoping to finish his work once things calmed down. The broker had been so busy that he had completely forgotten about his stash of stock orders.

The huge stock market crash of October 1929 resulted in the loss of $40 billion. It wiped out the savings of millions of investors, large and small. Some of the wealthiest investors lost millions. Professor Irving Fisher, who had expected the stock

Investors in London and other places around the world watched anxiously as U.S. stocks plummeted.

market to remain high forever, lost an estimated $10 million in the crash and was in debt for the rest of his life. Two members of the Marx Brothers comedy team, Groucho and Harpo, both lost much

of their wealth, too. Groucho later joked, "All I lost was $240,000. I would have lost more, but that was all the money I had."

The average small investor, while not losing such large dollar amounts, suffered more than wealthy investors. Nearly 1 million Americans had invested their life savings in the market. By the end of Black Tuesday, most of these small-time speculators—especially those who had bought stock on margin—had lost everything. Investors throughout the country and around the world no longer believed the stock market would recover.

Some people were so devastated by the events of Black Tuesday that they took their own lives. One such person was the head of the Union Cigar Company. When the value of his company's stock plummeted from $115 to $2, he jumped from the ledge of a New York building. One man in Milwaukee left a suicide note that read, "My body should go to science, my soul

DOCUMENTING U.S. HISTORY

In his book *Hard Times*, Studs Terkel recorded the stories of people who had lived through the stock market crash and the Great Depression. One of his subjects, Sidney J. Weinberg, who worked in finance, recalled: "I remember that day very intimately. I stayed in the office a week without going home. It must have been ten, eleven o'clock before we got the final reports. It was like a thunder clap. Everybody was stunned. Nobody knew what it was all about. ... I don't know anybody that jumped out of the window. But I know many who threatened to jump. They ended up in nursing homes and insane asylums and things like that. These were people who were trading in the market or in banking houses. They broke down physically as well as financially."

to Andrew W. Mellon [Hoover's secretary of the treasury], and sympathy to my creditors."

Men and women alike suffered under the stress and strain of losing their life savings. After the crash, New York hospitals reported an increase in female patients suffering from depression after losing their savings. Journalists of the 1920s estimated that about 20 percent of all small speculators were women.

Even Americans who had not gambled on the stock market suffered from the effects of the crash. The collapse of stocks caused people to lose confidence in the U.S. economy. Americans who had once boosted the economy by spending money freely now became more cautious than ever before. This, in turn, hurt companies that had continued producing goods for a booming economy.

Although no major banks failed after the crash, many smaller banks suffered. These banks had loaned out millions of dollars to brokers for margin accounts. Brokers had lent the money to investors using stock for collateral. The collateral on these loans was now worthless, and few people had the money to pay what they owed.

Financial experts continued to try to boost the market with their words. Some of the country's richest men joined in these efforts. The industrialist John D. Rockefeller, who had made his fortune in the oil industry, announced:

Believing that the fundamental conditions of the country are sound and that there is nothing in the business situation to warrant the destruction of values that has taken place ... my son and I have for some days been purchasing sound common stocks.

Financier John J. Raskob echoed Rockefeller's words, saying, "The pendulum has swung too far. The list is filled with bargains, and my friends and I are all buying stocks."

John D. Rockefeller tried to persuade investors that the economy was sound, but stocks continued to plummet.

New York City
Mayor Jimmy
Walker asked movie
theater operators not
to show newsreels
featuring images of
the crash.

Politicians weighed in, too. Mayor Jimmy Walker of New York City had a novel idea to help raise flagging confidence: "I appeal to movie exhibitors to show pictures that will reinstate courage and hopes in the hearts of the people."

Julius Klein, the assistant secretary of commerce, told the American people that they could help the economy by remaining positive:

> *There may be temporary recessions, but these can be reduced to a minimum if we all have confidence in the general upward trend. Many of the business recessions of past decades have been primarily psychological and could have been avoided or minimized if the businessmen and the masses of people had had the proper confidence in themselves.*

The calming reassurances of the experts worked yet again, and the stock market recovered slightly on Wednesday and Thursday. The NYSE closed early on Thursday and remained closed Friday and Saturday. The stock market crash was over, but that did not mean that a recovery was around the corner.

The Slow Slide Into Depression

Chapter

8

Although the panic was over, stocks had not yet reached the bottom. By November 13, three weeks after Black Tuesday, the market had fallen to its lowest point in 1929. By March 1930, nearly 2 million people were unemployed, many as a result of the crash.

The crash signaled the end of an era. The free-spending attitude and easygoing optimism that had marked the 1920s were gone. Contemporary historian Frederick Lewis Allen wrote:

> There was hardly a man or woman in the country whose attitude toward life had not been affected by it in some degree and was not now affected by the sudden and brutal shattering of hope.

During the Great Depression, unemployed Americans lined up for a bowl of hot soup or a loaf of bread.

The crash would forever be connected with the start of hard times in the minds of Americans across the nation. The Roaring Twenties were over; the Dirty Thirties had begun.

Financial experts could not agree on exactly what had caused the stock market crash in 1929. Today economists blame a number of different factors. One factor was the heavy speculation in the stock market that had driven the price of stocks

During the Great Depression, many investors lost their savings when banks, such as the American Union Bank in New York City, closed down.

far above their worth. Much of this speculation was made possible by the easy credit extended by banks and brokerages. Two other factors were the increase in investment trusts and the lack of federal laws to regulate the trusts. Finally, a sudden loss of confidence in the soundness of the economy and the market had played a role in the crash.

Government officials had a mixed response to the crash. Some even thought the collapse might be beneficial. Some years later, Herbert Hoover remembered:

> *Secretary of the Treasury Mellon felt that government must keep its hands off and let the slump liquidate itself. Mr. Mellon … held that even panic was not altogether a bad thing. He said: 'It will purge the rottenness out of the system. High costs of living and high living will come down. People will work harder, live a more moral life. Values will be adjusted, and enterprising people will pick up the wrecks from less competent people.'*

Although Hoover was later accused of inaction, the president did, in fact, act quickly to ease the effects of the stock market crash on Americans. He organized a meeting of the nation's top business leaders and recommended cuts in taxes and increased public works projects. The president believed that these actions were enough.

When he addressed the nation in December 1929, he told Americans:

> *I am convinced that through these measures we have reestablished confidence. Wages should remain stable. A very large degree of industrial unemployment and suffering which would otherwise have occurred has been prevented.*

Three months later, Hoover was still optimistic when he promised that the "worst effects of the crash upon unemployment will have passed during the next sixty days."

But the worst was not over. By 1931, the nation was firmly in the grip of the most serious economic crisis in its history. Hoover continued to believe that government had done all it should to aid those in trouble. He believed businesses, private charities, and individuals needed to step forward and find solutions to the crisis. In February 1931, Hoover told Americans:

> *We are going through a period when character and courage are on trial, and where the very faith that is within us is under test. Our people are meeting this test.*

As president during the 1929 stock market crash and the earliest days of the Great Depression, Hoover took much of the blame for the collapse of the U.S. economy. During the Great Depression, camps for homeless families in the United States were known as Hoovervilles. Hoover was overwhelmingly defeated during the presidential election of 1932 by Democratic candidate Franklin D. Roosevelt,

who offered a "new deal" for Americans. The New Deal was a series of social and economic policies and programs to help people who were suffering during the Great Depression. The Depression would continue throughout the 1930s, ending only after the United States entered World War II in 1941.

Presidential candidate Franklin D. Roosevelt promised Americans relief in the form of the New Deal.

Today most experts and historians agree that although the stock market crash of 1929 did not directly cause the Great Depression, it contributed to the country's economic crisis. Alex Samuels, a former college professor who became a farmer after the crash, related his views:

83

I don't believe that anyone thoroughly understands all of the causes of depressions. … Certainly Presidents Coolidge and Hoover did not understand the subject, or they would scarcely have allowed our present situation to develop while they smilingly assured the American people that all was well with the world and the best of our coming prosperity was just around the corner.

Today the stock market crash continues to fascinate economists and financial experts. People study the crash to learn more about how the economy and the stock market react to different types of pressures and events. Students of today's finances use the lessons learned from the 1929 market collapse to help them assess how the present stock market might behave. And people continue to question if such a catastrophic, or disastrous, event could ever occur again.

In 1987 a serious one-day crash caused financial analysts and historians to recall the 1929 crash. On Monday, October 19, stock values plummeted, causing a loss of about $500 billion. The event was the biggest single-day drop since 1914. After Black Monday, as the day became known, historians compared the most recent events with those of 1929. While the causes of the 1929 panic are well understood today, the exact causes of the rapid drop in stock values in 1987 remain a mystery to many financial experts. Another, smaller crash took place exactly 10 years later, and another in 2002.

Since 1929 the great stock market crash has become the symbol of a decadent era of free spending, changing social values, and uninvolved government. The disastrous crash marked an end to the newfound confidence and trust Americans had placed in political and business leaders. And it signaled the beginning of some of the darkest days in U.S. history. ◣

The stock market has grown and evolved as new technologies have developed.

85

Timeline

1790

The first stock exchange in the United States is founded in Philadelphia.

1792

A group of merchants on Wall Street in New York City sign the Buttonwood Agreement, founding the association that will become the New York Stock Exchange.

October 29, 1886

The first ticker tape parade takes place during the dedication of the Statue of Liberty.

1905

Henry Ford pioneers the assembly line, making mass production of automobiles possible.

1913

The U.S. Congress establishes the Federal Reserve Board to regulate the banking industry.

1918

World War I ends.

1920

Warren G. Harding, promising a return to normalcy, is elected as the 29th U.S. president.

1920

The 18th and 19th amendments to the Constitution are passed; the 18th Amendment makes Prohibition the law of the land; the 19th Amendment gives women across the nation the right to vote.

August 2, 1923

President Harding dies unexpectedly while on vacation; Vice President Calvin Coolidge is sworn in as the nation's 30th president.

November 1924

Coolidge is elected to a full term.

March 1928

The stock market enters its most profitable period ever, with more than 5 million stocks traded each day.

March 4, 1929

Herbert Hoover is inaugurated as the 31st U.S. president.

March 1929

Stock values drop; a record 8 million shares are traded in one day.

May 1929

Stock values again drop, but they recover in June.

Summer 1929

The New York Stock Exchange experiences record trading, and many stocks climb to an all-time high value.

August 1929

John J. Raskob, vice president of General Motors, writes an article about stock speculation titled "Everybody Ought to Be Rich."

September 3, 1929

The Dow Jones average reaches an all-time high.

September 5, 1929

A dip in the stock market known as the Babson Break takes places after a businessman makes a speech that forecasts trouble.

October 23, 1929

The stock market plummets as thousands of investors sell their stock.

October 24, 1929

On Black Thursday, panic spreads on Wall Street and around the nation as 12.9 million shares trade hands.

October 25–26, 1929

The stock market stabilizes after record losses in the previous days.

October 28, 1929

Massive sell-offs of stock continue; 9.2 million shares are traded in one day, about 3 million of which are sold in the last hour of business trading.

October 29, 1929, "Black Tuesday"

On Black Tuesday, the stock market reaches record lows as brokerage firms, banks, and companies dump stock onto the market.

10:30 A.M.

Within the first 30 minutes of trading, 3 million shares are traded.

3 P.M.

By the close of business trading, 16.4 million shares are sold.

November 13, 1929

The stock market falls to its lowest point of the year.

1932

As an economic depression grips the nation, Herbert Hoover loses his bid for re–election to Franklin D. Roosevelt.

On the Web

For more information on this topic, use FactHound.

1 Go to *www.facthound.com*

2 Type in this book ID: 0756533279

3 Click on the *Fetch It!* button. FactHound will find the best Web sites for you.

Historic Sites

New York Stock Exchange Building
11 Wall St.
New York, NY 10005

Visitors can see the building where the world's business is transacted and walk through the city's financial district.

Herbert Hoover National Historic Site
110 Parkside Drive
West Branch, IA 52358
319/643-2541

Visit the Herbert Hoover Presidential Library and Museum and the house where Hoover was born.

Look For More Books in This Series

The Berlin Wall:
Barrier to Freedom

A Day Without Immigrants:
Rallying Behind America's Newcomers

Freedom Rides:
Campaign for Equality

The March on Washington:
Uniting Against Racism

The National Grape Boycott:
A Victory for Farmworkers

The Teapot Dome Scandal:
Corruption Rocks 1920s America

Third Parties:
Influential Political Alternatives

A complete list of **Snapshots in History** titles is available on our Web site: *www.compasspointbooks.com*

Glossary

brokerage
company that specializes in buying and selling stocks for its customers

call loan
loan that must be paid back whenever the lender demands it

collateral
stocks, property, or other items used to guarantee payment of a loan

commodity
anything that can be bought or sold

depression
a period during which businesses, jobs, and stock values decline or stay low

Dow Jones average
daily list of the values of certain stocks

economy
the way a country produces, distributes, and uses its money, goods, natural resources, and services

financier
person whose job includes the handling of large sums of money

interest rate
fee charged to borrow money

investment trust
company that buys stocks in other companies in order to make money for its clients

investor
person who provides money for a project in return for a share in the profits

laissez-faire
principle of keeping government out of business and industry as much as possible

liquidate
to settle a debt by payment or other means

margin
buying of stocks on credit

New York Stock Exchange
in the early 1900s, the world's largest market for the buying and selling of stocks

Prohibition
laws against the production and sale of alcohol

recession
temporary slowing of business activity

securities
stock certificates

stock
the value of a company, divided into shares when sold to investors

stockbroker
person in charge of buying shares of a company

stock market
place where stocks are bought and sold

ticker tape machine
telegraph machine that printed out the latest value of important stocks on long, narrow strips of paper

Source Notes

Chapter 1

Page 8, line 7: "Gallery 6: The Great Depression." Herbert Hoover Presidential Library and Museum: Museum Galleries. 11 Dec. 2006. www.hoover.archives.gov/exhibits/Hooverstory/gallery06/gallery06.html.

Page 12, line 1: "R.V. Williams Interview with George Mehales, December 1938." December 1938. Library of Congress: American Memory. 11 Dec. 2006. www.memory.loc.gov

Page 13, line 4: "Bradley Interview with Raymond Tarver, January 5, 1940." 5 Jan. 1940. Library of Congress: American Memory. 11 Dec. 2006. www.memory.loc.gov

Page 13, line 15: "I was not thought clever enough." *Journal of the Churchill Centre & Societies* 124 (2004). Autumn 2004, p. 15.

Chapter 2

Page 16, line 1: F. Scott Fitzgerald. *The Crack-Up.* New York: New Directions Books, 1956, p. 30.

Page 21, line 1: George E. Mowry, ed. *The Twenties: Fords, Flappers, and Fanatics.* Englewood Cliffs, N.J.: Prentice-Hall, Inc, 1963, p. 179.

Page 21, line 8: Herman Bundesen. "Girl of Today Emancipated." (Originally printed in *Experience*, Vol. 2, No. 2, June 1924.) Flapper Jane. 11 Dec. 2006. www.flapperjane.com/April%202004/girl_of_today_emancipated.htm

Chapter 3

Page 26, line 12: Robert H. Ferrell and Howard H. Quint, eds. *The Talkative President: The Off-the-Record Press Conferences of Calvin Coolidge.* Amherst: University of Massachusetts Press, 1964, p. 19.

Page 27, line 4: Calvin Coolidge. "Inaugural Address, March 4, 1925." 4 March 1925. John F. Kennedy Library and Museum. 11 Dec. 2006. www.cs.umb.edu/~rwhealan/jfk/coolidge_inaugural.html

Page 27, line 14: Calvin Coolidge. "Speech to the American Society of Newspaper Editors Convention, January 17, 1925." 17 Jan. 1925. American Society of Newspaper Editors Convention. 11 Dec. 2006. www.asne.org/index.cfm?ID=46

Page 29, line 11: *The Twenties: Fords, Flappers, and Fanatics*, p. 32.

Page 32, sidebar: Ibid., p. 49.

Chapter 4
Page 41, line 1: Ibid., p. 38.

Page 42, line 11: Samuel Crowther. "Everybody Ought to be Rich: An Interview with John J. Raskob." *Ladies' Home Journal.* August 1929, pp. 8–9, 36.

Page 45, line 5: "William Jenkins Interview with Alex Samuels, December 15, 1939." 15 Dec. 1939. Library of Congress: American Memory. 11 Dec. 2006. www.memory.loc.gov

Chapter 5
Page 48, line 1: Frederick Lewis Allen. *Only Yesterday: An Informal History of the 1920s.* New York: HarperCollins, 2000, p. 263.

Page 50, line 7: Studs Terkel. *Hard Times: An Oral History of the Great Depression.* New York: New Press, 1970, p. 65.

Chapter 6
Page 54, line 13: Maury Klein. *Rainbow's End: The Crash of 1929.* New York: Oxford University Press, 2001, p. 13.

Page 56, line 3: Ibid., pp. 194–195.

Page 57, line 14: *Only Yesterday: An Informal History of the 1920s,* p. 282.

Page 57, line 18: William Norman Grigg. "Criminalizing Capitalism." *The New American* Vol. 18, No. 17. 26 Aug. 2002. 11 Dec. 2006. www.thenewamerican. com/tna/2002/08-26-2002/vo18no17_capitalism.htm

Page 57, line 25: *Only Yesterday: An Informal History of the 1920s,* p. 281.

Page 58, line 4: Ibid., p. 280.

Page 58, sidebar: *Rainbow's End: The Crash of 1929,* p. 193.

Page 62, line 3: *Only Yesterday: An Informal History of the 1920s,* p. 287.

Page 63, line 8: Ibid., p. 289.

Page 63, line 16: "Caution Advised by Stockbrokers." *The New York Times.* 25 Oct. 1929, pp. 2, 26.

Page 63, line 23: Ibid.

Page 64, line 3: Ibid.

Page 65, line 3: *Only Yesterday: An Informal History of the 1920s,* pp. 280–281.

Source Notes

Chapter 7

Page 69, line 5: "Closing Rally Vigorous." *The New York Times*. 30 Oct. 1929, p. 1.

Page 69, line 9: Ibid., p. 3.

Page 69, sidebar: "Women Traders Going Back to Bridge Games; Say They Are Through With Stocks Forever." *The New York Times*. 30 Oct. 1929. New York Times on the Web. 11 Dec. 2006. www.nytimes.com/library/financial/103029crash-women.html

Page 73, line 1: *Rainbow's End: The Crash of 1929*, p. 231.

Page 73, line 30: William K. Klingaman. *1929: The Year of the Great Crash*. New York: Harper and Row, 1989, p. 297.

Page 73, sidebar: *Hard Times: An Oral History of the Great Depression,* pp. 72–73.

Page 75, line 1: *Only Yesterday: An Informal History of the 1920s*, p. 292.

Page 75, line 8: *Rainbow's End: The Crash of 1929,* p. 230

Page 76, line 3: Gordon Thomas and Max Morgan-Witts. *The Day the Bubble Burst: A Social History of the Wall Street Crash of 1929*. Garden City, N.Y.: Doubleday & Company, 1979, p. xv.

Page 77, line 4: "Closing Rally Vigorous."

Chapter 8

Page 78, line 11: *Only Yesterday: An Informal History of the 1920s,* p. 294.

Page 81, line 12: J. Bradford DeLong. "The Great Crash and the Great Slump." University of California at Berkeley Economist Brad DeLong Home Page: Slouching Towards Utopia?: The Economic History of the Twentieth Century. 11 Dec. 2006. http://econ161.berkeley.edu/TCEH/Slouch_Crash14.html

Page 82, line 1: Herbert Hoover. "State of the Union Address, December 3, 1929." 3 Dec. 1929. The American Presidency Project. 11 Dec. 2006. www.presidency.ucsb.edu/ws/index.php?pid=22021

Page 82, line 7: Colin Gordon, ed. *Major Problems in American History. 1920–1945.* Boston: Houghton Mifflin, 1999, p. 200.

Page 82, line 18: Ibid., p. 185.

Page 84, line 1: "William Jenkins Interview with Alex Samuels, December 15, 1939."

Select Bibliography

Allen, Frederick Lewis. *Only Yesterday: An Informal History of the 1920s.* New York: HarperCollins, 2000.

Gordon, Colin, ed. *Major Problems in American History, 1920–1945.* Boston: Houghton Mifflin, 1999.

Klein, Maury. *Rainbow's End: The Crash of 1929.* New York: Oxford University Press, 2001.

Klingaman, William K. *1929: The Year of the Great Crash.* New York: Harper and Row, 1989.

Kyvig, David E. *Daily Life in the United States, 1920–1940.* Chicago: Ivan R. Dee, 2002.

Parrish, Michael E. *Anxious Decades: America in Prosperity and Depression, 1920–1941.* New York: W.W. Norton & Company, 1992.

Thomas, Gordon, and Max Morgan-Witts. *The Day the Bubble Burst: A Social History of the Wall Street Crash of 1929.* Garden City, N.Y.: Doubleday & Company, 1979.

Further Reading

Fuller, Donna Jo. *The Stock Market.* Minneapolis: Lerner Publications, 2006.

Feinberg, Barbara. *Black Tuesday: The Stock Market Crash of 1929.* Brookfield, Conn.: Millbrook Press, 1995.

Freedman, Russell. *Children of the Great Depression.* New York: Clarion, 2005.

Gilman, Laura Anne. *Economics: How Economics Works.* Minneapolis: Lerner Publications, 2005.

Kendall, Martha E. *Herbert Hoover: America's 31st President.* Danbury, Conn.: Children's Press, 2004.

Terkel, Studs. *Hard Times: An Oral History of the Great Depression.* New York: The New Press, 2000.

Index

ABOUT THE AUTHOR

Robin S. Doak is a writer and former editor of *Weekly Reader* and *U*S*Kids* magazine. She has written many nonfiction books for children. She lives with her husband, two children, two dogs, and two cats in central Connecticut.

IMAGE CREDITS

Corbis, **cover**, pp. **9, 11** and **back cover (left), 15, 20, 22, 30–31, 34, 49, 55, 60, 64, 67, 68, 72, 76, 80, 86** (bottom left) (Bettmann), **85** (Reuters) **29** (Swim Ink 2, LLC), **33** (Wolff & Tritschler/zefa), **47** and **back cover (middle), 62, 75**; Getty Images, pp. **71, 83**; Library of Congress pp. **17, 19, 25, 42–43, 2** and **50, 86** (top right); TopFoto, pp. **5** and **37, 6** and **39, 59, 79** and **back cover (right), 87** (both) (Topham Picturepoint), **44** (Roger-Viollet)